The Batter's Out
(Baseball Training Manual)

How to Play Defense: For Parents, Coaches, and Kids

Charles R. Sledge Jr.

AuthorHouse™
1663 Liberty Drive, Suite 200
Bloomington, IN 47403
www.authorhouse.com
Phone: 1-800-839-8640

First published by AuthorHouse 7/2/2008

ISBN: 978-1-4343-4364-2 (sc)

Printed in the United States of America
Bloomington, Indiana

This book is printed on acid-free paper.

authorHOUSE®

Subscribers

1. Clayvon R. Sledge

2. Chuck Lewis JR.

3. Carol A. Rector

4. Valisa Dutrieuille

5. Demetrius, Amon, & Niyah Baldwin-Youngblood

6. De Vaughn Robinson

7. Edwina Ramsey (Andy Buxton)

8. Mr. & Mrs. Nathanial Carter Sr. & Family

9. Rondaya Brown

10. Richard Lindsay and Family

11. Elder Bernard Carter Sr. & Family

12. Raymar, Valerie, Deseray, & Jordyn Hester

This book is dedicated to my mother Carol who has always encouraged me to become an artist as well as a baseball player. Also, to my wife Gwendolyn, my Children Charles III, Carlos, Charise, and Clayvon who I love and all support me. To all those who came through the years of playing and coaching baseball, and to all who dream to one day play professional baseball.

Contents

THE POSITION OF PLAYERS GUIDE

The Pitcher no. 1

The Catcher no. 2

The First Baseman no. 3

The Second Baseman no. 4

The Third Baseman no. 5

The Shortstop no. 6

The Left Fielder no. 7

The Center Fielder no. 8

The Right Fielder no. 9

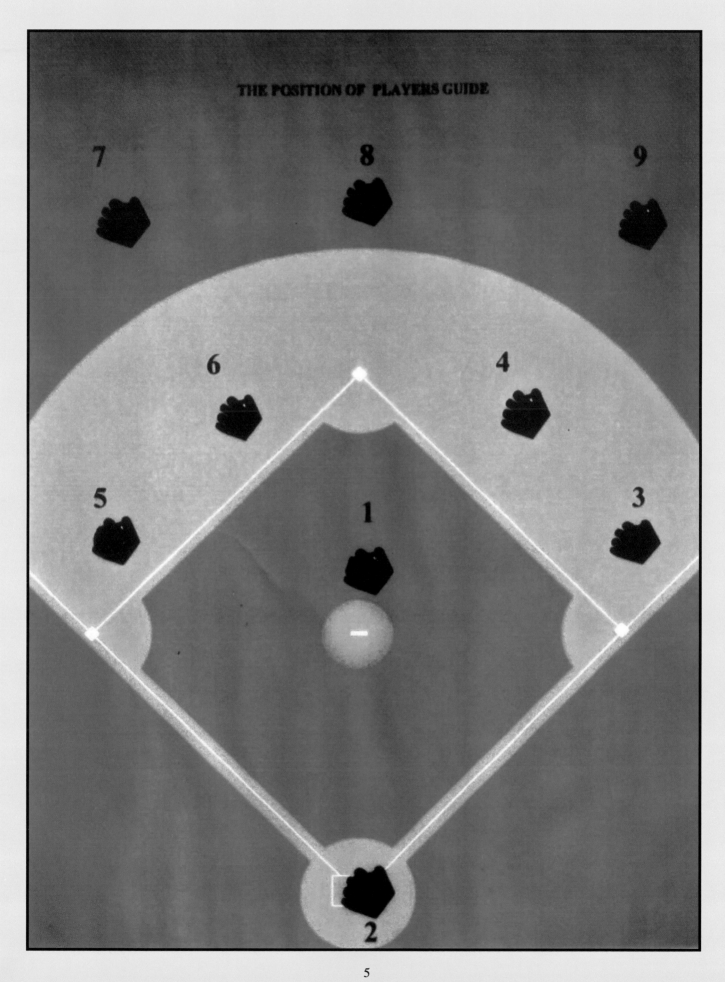

THE POSITION OF PLAYERS GUIDE

THE BALL HIT TO THE PITCHER

When the ball is hit, the **Pitcher** should field the ball and throw it to the **First Baseman** who should be covering first base. If the ball is being thrown away at first base and seeing that the **Catcher** is running to back up first base, the **Pitcher** should at that time cover home plate. (**Note:** the **Catcher** only backs up first base when the ball is hit to the **Pitcher** or towards the left side of the infield and there are no runners on base.)

The Catcher should run to back up first base as soon as the **Pitcher** fields the ball and makes his throw to first base. **The Pitcher** may possibly throw the ball away at first base and the **Catcher** might have to field the ball as the back up and make his throw towards second base.

The First Baseman should move to step on first base and wait to catch the ball thrown by the **Pitcher.**

The Second Baseman should run behind second base backing up the **Pitcher. The Shortstop** should be covering second base. **The Pitcher** may miss the ball, or else throw the ball away at first base once he fields it. The runner could be advancing in the direction of second base.

The Third Baseman should move in the direction of the ball in case the **Pitcher** fields or misses it, then he runs to cover third base when the **Pitcher** fields the ball.

The Shortstop also, should move towards the ball in case the **Pitcher** fields or misses it, and then he should cover second base when the **Pitcher** fields the ball.

The Left Fielder should run towards the ball backing up the **Pitcher** and the **Center Fielder.** As soon as the **Pitcher** fields the ball and makes his throw to first base he then runs to back up third base.

The **Center Fielder** should run towards the ball (in case it gets past the **Pitcher, Second Baseman,** or the **Shortstop**) backing up the **Second Baseman,** who should be backing up the **Shortstop,** who should back up the **Pitcher** while covering second base.

The **Right Fielder** should run in to back up first base as soon as the **Pitcher** fields the ball. **The Pitcher** might throw the ball away at first base, and the **Right Fielder** may possibly field the ball as the back up and make his throw towards second base.

NOTES:

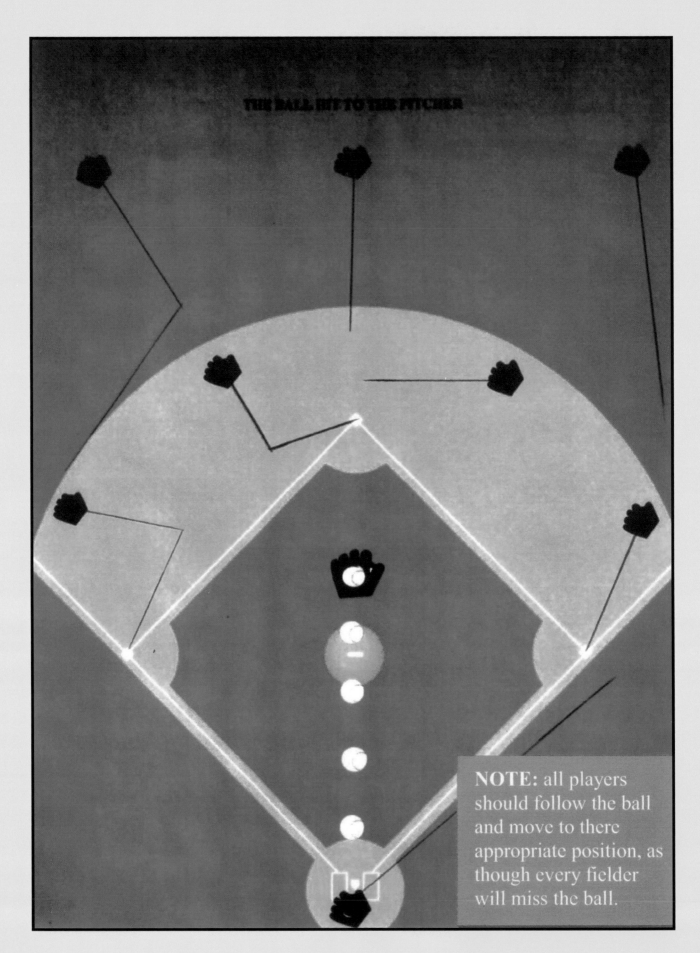

THE BALL HIT TO THE CATCHER'S LEFT SIDE

When the ball is being hit to the **Catcher's** left side, the **Pitcher** should charge the ball after seeing the ball being hit out in front of home plate down the third base line.

The **Catcher** also, charges the ball hit to the left side of the infield out in front of home plate down the third base line. He may have to field the ball and throw it to the **First Baseman** who should be covering first base.

The **First Baseman** should move to cover first base, step on the base, and wait to catch the ball thrown by the **Pitcher, Catcher,** or the **Third Baseman.**

The **Second Baseman** should move to cover second base when the batter hits the ball to the **Catcher's** left side.

The **Third Baseman** charges the ball hit down the third base line in front of the **Catcher. The Third Baseman** may possibly have to field the ball and throw it to the **First Baseman** who should be covering first base.

The **Shortstop** should move to cover third base as soon as the **Third Baseman** charges the ball hit down the third base line.

The **Left Fielder** charges in to back up the **Shortstop** who should be moving to cover third base. The ball may be thrown away at first base by the **Pitcher, Catcher,** or the **Third Baseman** and the **Right Fielder,** who backs up first base, may have to field the ball and make a throw towards second base or across the field to third base.

The Center Fielder should run towards the ball backing up the **Second Baseman** who should be covering second base. The ball may be thrown away at first base by an infielder, and the player **(The Right Fielder)** who backs up first base might have to make a throw towards second base and the **Second baseman** may miss the ball.

The Right Fielder charges in to back up first base for the **First Baseman** in case the ball is thrown away at first base by the **Pitcher, Catcher,** or the **Third Baseman.**

NOTES:

THE BALL HIT TO THE CATCHER'S RIGHT SIDE

Once the **Pitcher** sees that the ball is being hit to the **Catcher's** right side, he should charge the ball hit anywhere down the first, or third base line out in front of home plate.

The **Catcher** also, charges the ball hit down the first or third base line out in front of home plate, since he may have to field the ball and throw it to the **Second Baseman** who should be covering first base.

The **First Baseman** charges the ball hit in front of the **Catcher** down the first base line. If the **First Baseman** reaches the ball before the **Catcher,** the **First Baseman** should throw the ball to the **Second Baseman** who should be covering first base.

The **Second Baseman** should run over to first base, steps on the base, and waits to catch the ball thrown by the **Pitcher, Catcher,** or the **First Baseman.**

The **Third Baseman** should move to third base, cover the base, and wait for a play.

The **Shortstop** should move to cover second base, while the **Second Baseman** moves to cover first base, and wait for a play.

The **Left Fielder** should run in the direction of second base backing up the **Shortstop** who should be covering that base. The ball may be thrown away at first base by the **Pitcher, Catcher,** or the **First baseman.** If the ball is missed at first base by the **Second Baseman** the runner could be on his way towards second base. **The Right Fielder,** who backs up first base, may possibly field the ball and throw it to the **Shortstop,** who should be covering second base.

The **Center Fielder** should run to back up the **Right Fielder,** who should be there backing up the **Second Baseman,** who should be covering first base. The ball may be thrown away at first base by the **Pitcher, Catcher,** or the **First Baseman,** and the **Second Baseman** who should cover first base, or the **Right Fielder** who should back up first base, may field or miss the ball.

The **Right Fielder** charges in to back up the **Second Baseman** who should be covering first base. The ball could be thrown away at first base by an infielder. **The Right Fielder** may possibly field the ball as the back up and throw it to the **Shortstop,** who should be covering second base.

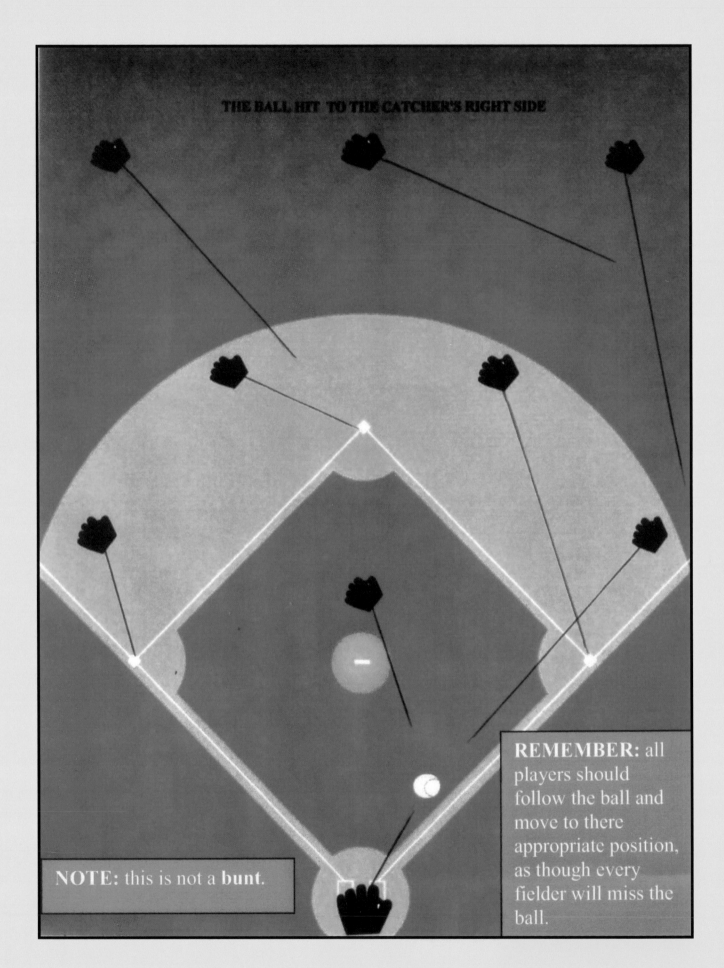

THE BALL HIT TO THE FIRST BASEMAN

The Pitcher should run over to assist first base at all times when the ball is hit towards the right side of the infield to either the **First,** or **Second Baseman.**

The Catcher has to stay at home plate to stop a runner from scoring.

The First Baseman should field the ball and step on first base before the runner to receive an out.

The Second Baseman should run over to first base for back up and to assist the **First Baseman** in case he fields or misses the ball.

The Third Baseman should move to cover third base and wait for a play.

The Shortstop should move to second base, cover the base, and wait for a play.

The Left Fielder should run towards second base to back up the **Shortstop** who should be covering second base when the batter hits the ball to the **First Baseman.**

The Center Fielder should run in the direction of the **Right Fielder** (who is backing up first base) to back him up in case the ball is missed at first base by the **First Baseman,** and the **Right Fielder** misses it as well.

The Right Fielder should run in to back up the **First Baseman** who should field the ball. If the ball is missed at first base by the **First Baseman,** the **Second Baseman** or the **Right Fielder,** who both should back up first base, may have to field the ball and throw it to the **Shortstop** who should be covering second base. The runner could be trying to advance one more base.

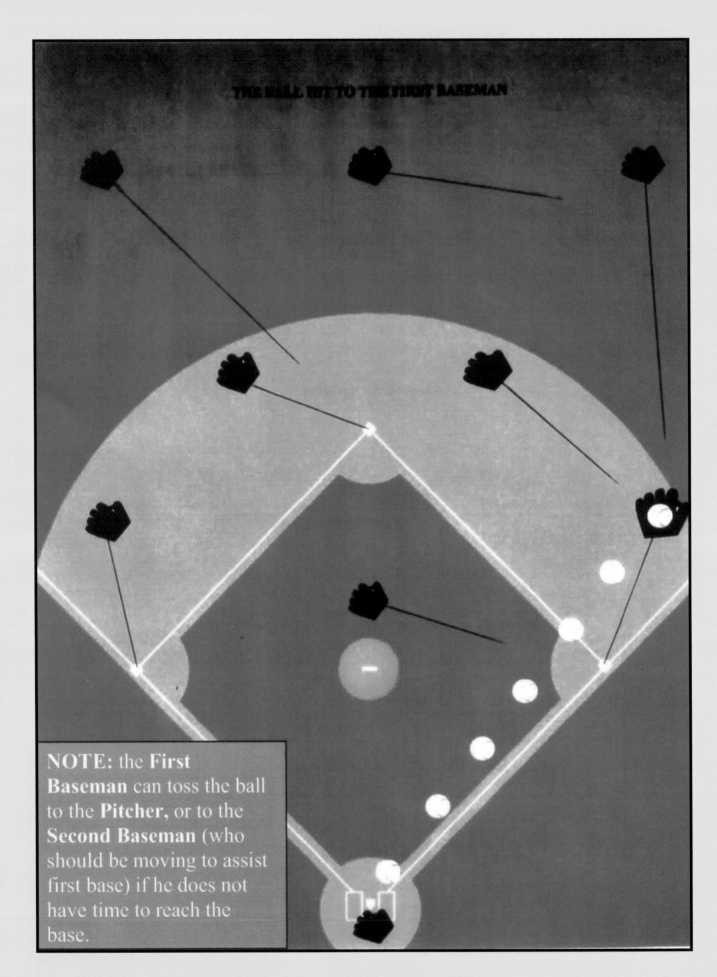

NOTE: the **First Baseman** can toss the ball to the **Pitcher,** or to the **Second Baseman** (who should be moving to assist first base) if he does not have time to reach the base.

THE BALL HIT TO THE SECOND BASEMAN

The Pitcher should run to assist first base when the ball is hit to the right side of the infield to either the **First,** or **Second Baseman** at all times**.**

The Catcher has to stay at home plate to stop a runner from scoring.

The First Baseman should cover first base, step on the base, and wait to catch the ball thrown by the **Second Baseman** who should field the ball.

The Second Baseman should field the ball and throw it to the **First Baseman** who should be covering first base.

The Third Baseman should move to cover third base and wait for a play.

The Shortstop should move to cover second base and wait for a play. The ball may be thrown away at first base by the **Second Baseman** once he fields the ball and makes his throw. **The Catcher** or the **Right Fielder,** who both should be backing up first base, may have to field the ball and throw it to the **Shortstop** who should be covering second base. The runner may possibly be trying to advance towards second base.

As soon as the ball is hit to the **Second Baseman,** the **Left Fielder** should run in the direction of second base to back up the **Shortstop** who should be covering second base. **The Second Baseman** may field the ball and throw it away at first base. This will allow the runner to advance towards second base.

The **Center Fielder** should run towards the ball behind the **Second Baseman** in case he fields or misses the ball. Once fielded by the **Second Baseman**, the **Center Fielder** should then run to the left field side of second base as the back up. The ball may be thrown away at first base by the **Second Baseman** and the runner may possibly try to advance one more base.

The **Right Fielder** also, runs towards the ball backing up the **Second Baseman** in case he fields or misses the ball. Once the ball is fielded by the **Second Baseman,** the **Right Fielder** should move to back up first base for the reason that the **Second Baseman** may throw the ball away at first base.

NOTES:

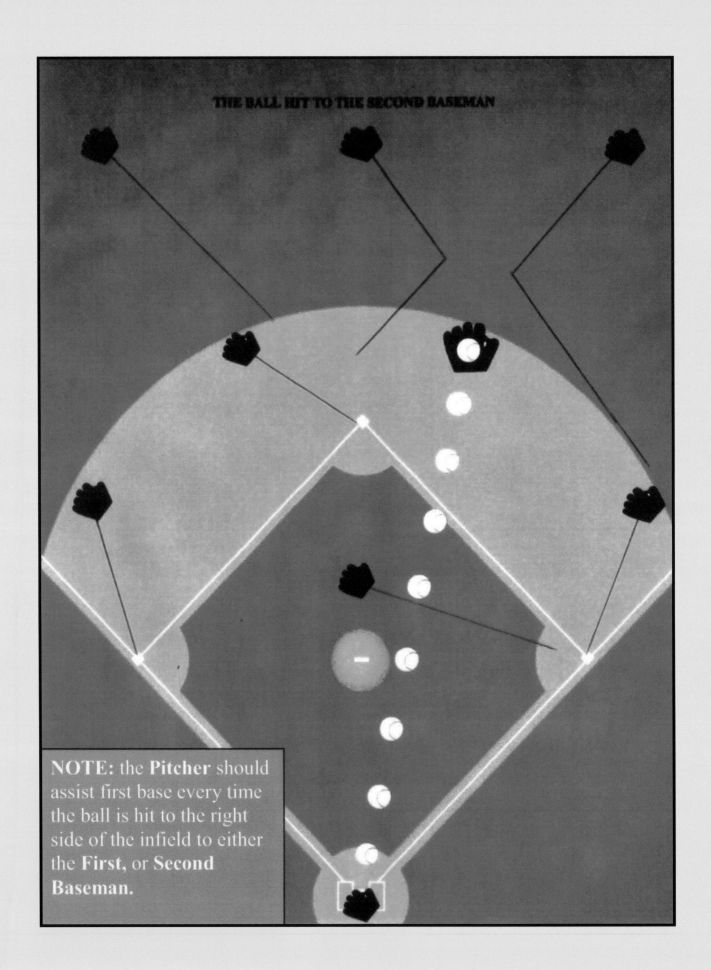

THE BALL HIT TO THE SECOND BASEMAN

NOTE: the **Pitcher** should assist first base every time the ball is hit to the right side of the infield to either the **First,** or Second **Baseman.**

THE BALL HIT TO THE THIRD BASEMAN

When the ball is hit to the **Third Baseman,** the **Pitcher** should cover home plate (to stop a runner from scoring) at the same time the **Catcher** runs to back up first base.

The Catcher should run to back up first base in case the **Third Baseman** fields the ball and he throws it away at first base. **The Catcher** only backs up first base when the ball is being hit to the **Pitcher** or to the left side of the infield to the **Shortstop,** or to the **Third Baseman** and there are no runners on base.

The First Baseman should cover first base, step on the base, and wait to catch the ball thrown by the **Third Baseman.**

The Second Baseman should move to cover second base and wait for a play. The runner on his way to first base could be trying to advance one more base if the ball is thrown away at first base by the **Third Baseman.**

The Third Baseman should field the ball and throw it to the **First Baseman** who should be covering first base. Once he fields the ball and makes his throw to first base, the **Shortstop** at that time should cover third base.

The Shortstop should run towards the ball backing up the **Third Baseman** in case he fields or misses the ball. Once fielded by the **Third Baseman,** the **Shortstop** at that time should cover third base.

The Left Fielder should run towards the ball and third base backing up the **Third Baseman** in case he fields or misses the ball. If the ball is missed at third base, the **Left Fielder** should field the ball as the back up and throw it to the **Second Baseman** who should be covering second base. If the **Left Fielder** has any trouble fielding the ball, it should be thrown to the **Shortstop** who should be acting as the cut-off man once the ball is missed at third base.

The Center Fielder should run over to left field as the back up in case the ball is missed by the **Third Baseman** as well as the **Left Fielder.** Once fielded by the **Third Baseman,** the **Center Fielder** should charge in the direction of second base for back up in case the **Third Baseman** throws the ball away at first base. The runner on first base could be trying to advance one more base.

The Right Fielder should run in to back up the **First Baseman** in case the ball is thrown away at first base by the **Third Baseman** who may field the ball. If the ball is missed at third base, the **Right Fielder** should look to back up second base since the ball should be thrown into second base from left field.

NOTES:

22

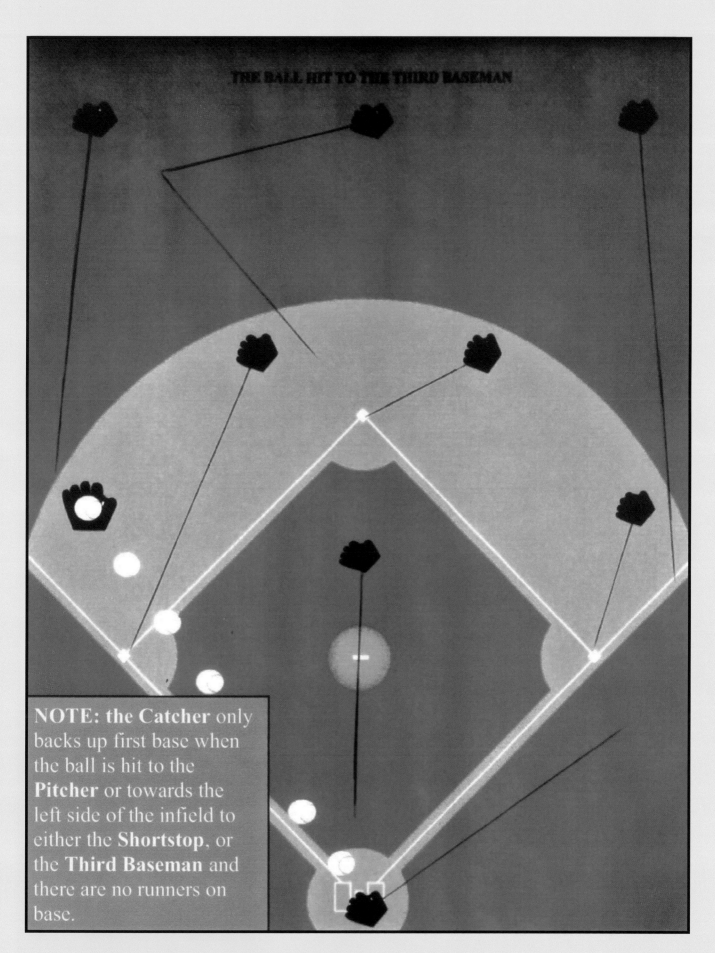

THE BALL HIT TO THE THIRD BASEMAN

NOTE: the Catcher only backs up first base when the ball is hit to the Pitcher or towards the left side of the infield to either the Shortstop, or the Third Baseman and there are no runners on base.

THE BALL HIT TO THE SHORTSTOP

When the ball is hit to the **Shortstop,** the **Pitcher** should run to cover home plate as soon as the **Catcher** moves to back up first base. **The Catcher** only backs up first base when the ball is hit to the **Pitcher** or to the left side of the infield and there are no runners on base.

The Catcher should run up the first base line as the back up to first base, along with the **Right Fielder** running in from right field. **The First Baseman** should be covering first base. The ball could be thrown away at first base by the **Shortstop,** and the **Catcher,** or the **Right Fielder** may have to field the ball as the back up and throw it to the **Second Baseman** who should be covering second base.

The First Baseman should covers first base, step on the base, and wait to catch the ball thrown by the **Shortstop.**

The Second Baseman should move to cover second base and wait for a play.

The Third Baseman should run towards the ball backing up the **Shortstop** in case he fields or misses the ball. He then covers third base as soon as the **Shortstop** fields the ball and makes his throw to first base. Depending upon the speed or location of the ball hit to the **Shortstop,** the **Third Baseman** may perhaps get (in the hole) to the ball and field it before the **Shortstop.**

The Shortstop should field the ball and throw it to the **First Baseman** who should be covering first base.

The **Left Fielder** should run towards the ball behind the **Shortstop** as the back up in case he fields or misses the ball. Once the ball is fielded, the **Left Fielder** should be in the position to back up second base given that the **Shortstop** may throw the ball away at first base. The runner could be trying to advance to the next base.

The **Center Fielder** also, runs towards the ball behind the **Shortstop** for back up in case he fields or misses the ball. **The Center Fielder** should then move behind the left field side of second base for back up when the **Shortstop** fields it. The ball could be thrown away at first base by the **Shortstop** and the runner could be trying to advance towards second base.

The **Right Fielder** should run in to back up first base (along with the **Catcher**) in case the ball is thrown away at first by the **Shortstop. The Right Fielder** may possibly field the ball as the back up and throw it to the **Second Baseman** who should be covering second base. The runner could be trying to advance one more base.

NOTES:

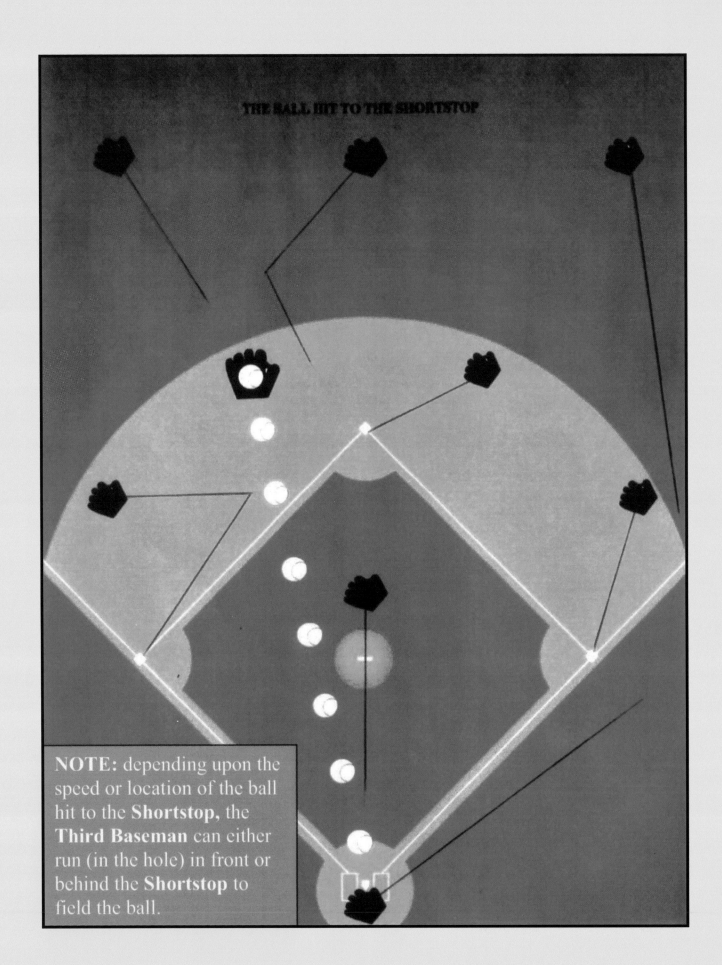

THE BALL HIT TO THE LEFT FIELDER

When the ball is hit to the **Left Fielder,** the **Pitcher** should move to position himself in between home plate and the player fielding the ball in left field. The ball may be missed in left field and the **Pitcher** may possibly have to line up the throw from left field into home plate if necessary.

The Catcher has to stay at home plate to stop a runner from scoring and to help the **Pitcher** position himself in between home plate, and the player fielding the ball in left field, lining up the throw into home plate by communicating, saying to the **Pitcher** "left or right".

The First Baseman should cover first base and wait for a throw to be made from the **Second Baseman** behind the runner who has just rounded first base heading back towards first.

The Second Baseman should cover second base, line up the throw, and catch the ball thrown in from left field or from the **Shortstop** who acts as the cut-off man. The **Second Baseman** should help line up the throw into second base by communicating, saying to the **Shortstop** "left or right". The runner on first base could be trying to advance towards second base and a good throw is needed to get the runner out.

The Third Baseman should move to cover third base and wait for a play.

The Shortstop should position himself between the **Left Fielder** who may field the ball and second base. **The Shortstop** acts as the cut-off man to line up the throw into second base from left field.

The Left Fielder should field the ball and throw it to the **Second Baseman** who should be covering second base. If the **Left Fielder** has any trouble fielding the ball it should be thrown to the **Shortstop** who acts as the cut-off man lining up the throw.

The Center Fielder should run in the direction of left field backing up the **Left Fielder** in case he fields or misses the ball. Once the ball is fielded by an outfielder, it should be thrown to the **Second Baseman** who should be covering second base. If an outfielder has any trouble fielding the ball it should be thrown to the **Shortstop** who acts as the cut-off man lining up the throw.

The Right Fielder should run in the direction of second base backing up the **Second Baseman. The Second Baseman,** who should be covering second base, may miss the ball when it is thrown in from left field.

NOTES:

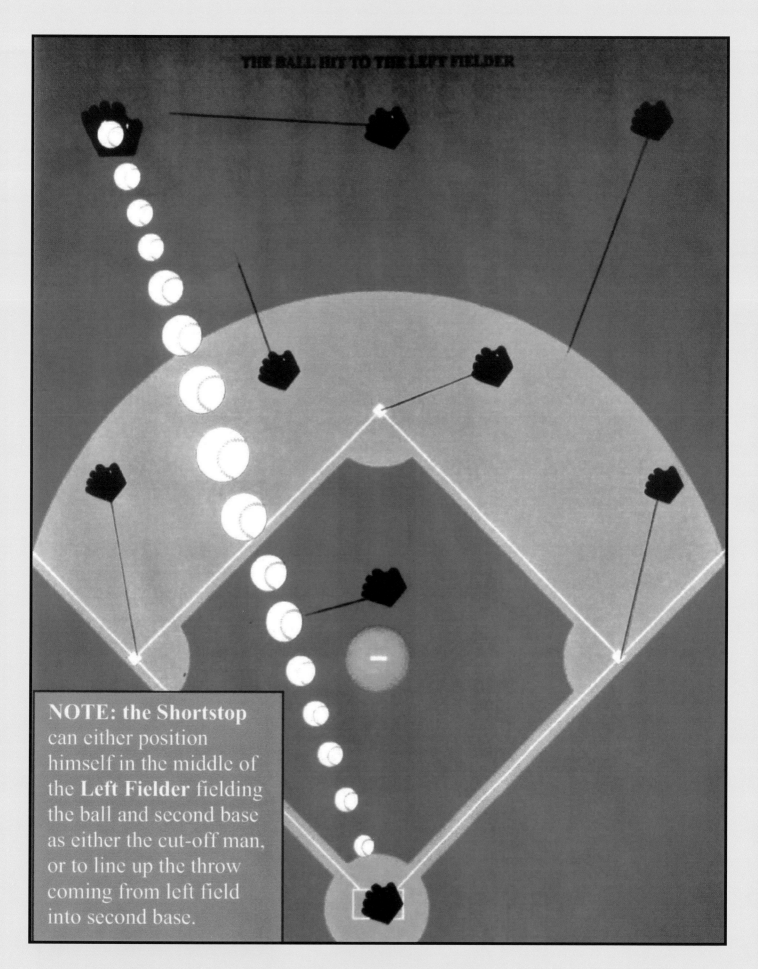

THE BALL HIT TO THE LEFT FIELDER

NOTE: the Shortstop can either position himself in the middle of the **Left Fielder** fielding the ball and second base as either the cut-off man, or to line up the throw coming from left field into second base.

THE BALL HIT TO THE CENTER FIELDER

When the ball is hit to the **Center Fielder,** the **Pitcher** should move behind second base for back up as soon as the ball is thrown into second base from center field. The ball could be missed at second base by the **Shortstop,** or the **Second Baseman,** who may be covering second base depending on which side of second base the ball is hit on, the left field side, or the right field side of the base. **The Pitcher** also, acts as the cut-off man to line up the throw into home plate from center field if necessary.

The Catcher has to stay at home plate to stop a runner from scoring and to help the **Pitcher** line up the throw into home plate by positioning him in between home plate, and the player fielding the ball in center field by communicating, saying to the **Pitcher** "left or right".

.

The First Baseman should move to cover first base and wait for a play. The runner may possibly be rounding first base and the ball could be thrown (by the **Second Baseman/Shortstop**) behind the runner who is heading back towards first.

Depending upon which side of second base the ball is hit on, the left field side, or the right field side, the **Second Baseman** who covers the right side of the infield should either catch the ball thrown in from center field as the cut-off man, or cover second base when the ball is hit to the left field side of the **Center Fielder.**

The Third Baseman should move to cover third base and wait for a play.

Depending upon which side of second base the ball is hit on, the left field side, or the right field side, the **Shortstop** who covers the left side of the infield should either catch the ball thrown in from center field as the cut-off man, or cover second base when the ball is hit to the right field side of the **Center Fielder.**

The Left Fielder should run towards the ball backing up the **Center Fielder** in case he fields or misses the ball.

Depending upon which side of second base the ball is hit on, the left field side, or the right field side, the **Center Fielder** should field the ball and throw it to second base, **(Second Baseman/ Shortstop)** or to the cut-off man **(Shortstop/ Second Baseman)** if he has any trouble fielding the ball. This is where communication becomes real important.

The Right Fielder should run towards the ball in the direction of the **Center Fielder** as the back up in case he fields or misses the ball. Once the ball is fielded, it should be thrown into second base from the outfield, or if the outfielder has any trouble fielding the ball it should be thrown to the cut-off man.

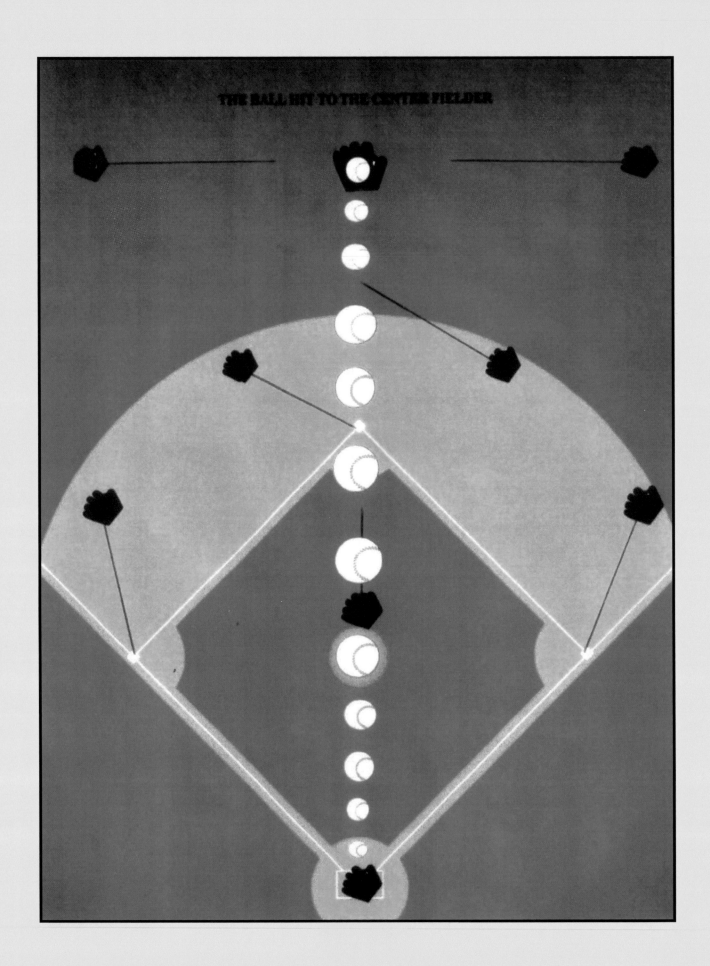

THE BALL HIT TO THE CENTER FIELDER

THE BALL HIT TO THE RIGHT FIELDER

When the ball is hit to the **Right Fielder,** the **Pitcher** should position himself between home plate and the player fielding the ball in right field, to line up the throw from right field into home plate if necessary. The ball may perhaps get past the **Right Fielder** and the **Center Fielder,** and a good throw is needed to stop the runner from scoring.

The Catcher has to stay at home plate to stop a runner from scoring and to help the **Pitcher** position himself in between home plate and the player fielding the ball in right field, lining up the throw into home plate by communicating, saying to the **Pitcher** "left or right".

.

The First Baseman should move to cover first base and wait for a throw to come behind the runner (who has rounded first base heading back towards the base) from the **Shortstop**.

The Second Baseman should position himself between the **Right Fielder** who may field the ball and second base as the cut-off man, to line up the throw from right field into second base.

The Third Baseman should move to cover third base and wait for a play.

The Shortstop should move to cover second base and wait to catch the ball thrown in from right field, or from the **Second Baseman** who should be the cut-off man lining up the throw.

The Left Fielder should run in backing up the **Shortstop** who should be covering second base. **The Right Fielder,** who should field the ball, may throw the ball away at second base and the **Shortstop,** who should be covering second base, could miss the ball.

The Center Fielder should run towards right field backing up the **Right Fielder** in case he fields or misses the ball. Once the ball is fielded, it should be thrown into second base, or if an outfielder has trouble fielding the ball, it should be thrown to the cut-off man.

The Right Fielder should field the ball and throw it to the **Shortstop** who should be covering second base. If the **Right Fielder** has trouble fielding the ball it should be thrown to the **Second Baseman** who should be the cut-off man lining up the throw once the ball is fielded.

REMEMBER: any time an outfielder has trouble fielding the ball, it should be thrown to the cut-off man for the reason that the runner may be trying to advance to another base and the throw may be too late.

NOTES:

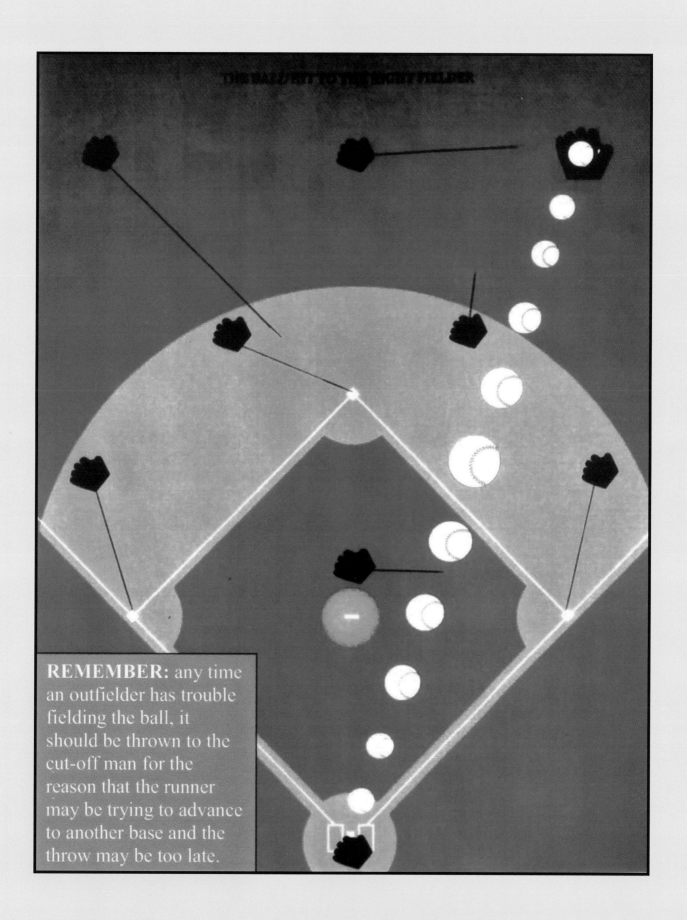

REMEMBER: any time an outfielder has trouble fielding the ball, it should be thrown to the cut-off man for the reason that the runner may be trying to advance to another base and the throw may be too late.

THE BUNT

The Pitcher charges towards home plate almost immediately after a pitch.

The Catcher charges the ball **bunted** out in front of home plate and down the first or third base line when there are no runners on base.

The First Baseman charges towards home plate as soon as the batter squares around to **bunt** the ball when there are no runners on base.

The Second Baseman should run to cover first base, steps on the base, and waits to catch the ball thrown by the **Pitcher, Catcher, First,** or the **Third Baseman.**

The Third Baseman charges towards home plate as soon as the batter squares around to **bunt** the ball when there are no runners on base.

The Shortstop should move to cover second base and wait for a play. The ball may be coming back towards second base if it is thrown away at first base.

The Left fielder charges in to cover third base (to protect a base from being open) seeing that the **Third Baseman** charges the **bunt.**

The Center Fielder charges in to back up the **Shortstop** who should be covering second base at the time the ball is **bunted.**

The Right Fielder charges in to back up the **Second Baseman** who should be covering first base as soon as the ball is **bunted.** The ball could be thrown away at first base by the **Pitcher, Catcher, First Baseman,** and/or the **Third Baseman. The Right Fielder** may have to field the ball as the back up and throw it to second or third base.

NOTES:

NOTE: Notice that this is a **Bunt** without any runners on base. **The Pitcher** has the view of the ball and home plate. **The Catcher** has the view of the ball and all three bases. **The First Baseman** has the view of the ball, third base, and home plate. **The Third Baseman** has the view of the ball, home plate, and first base. The ball should be fielded by either the **Catcher** or the **Third Baseman** if possible.

REMEMBER: the base to throw the ball depends on who fields the ball, which base is occupied, and how many outs are there.

REMEMBER:

WHO'S ON WHAT BASE,

HOW MANY OUTS ARE THERE,

AND WHAT AM I GOING TO DO

WHEN I GET TO THE BALL?

GLOSSARY

1. **ALL -** Representing the entire or total number of quantity.

2. **ASSIST -** To give help or support, to be present.

3. **BACK UP -** Someone who takes the place of another when things get dangerous or difficult.

4. **BASE - a.** This is the starting point, or a safety area on a baseball field.
   b. Any one of the four corners of an infield marked by a bag or plate that must be touched by a runner before a run can be scored.

5. **BASEBALL - a.** A game played with a bat, and ball by two opposing teams of nine players, each team playing alternately in the field and at bat.
   b. The players at bat having to run a course of four bases laid out in a diamond pattern in order to score.

6. **BATTER -** A player who is batting.

7. **BEHIND -** In a position, or attitude of support.

8. **BUNT - a.** To bat a ball by tapping it lightly so that the ball roles slowly in front of the infielders.

9. **CATCH - a.** To grab; to stop the motion of or, to catch a ball.
   b. To reach just in time.

10. **CATCHER -** Plays behind the plate.

11. **CENTER FIELDER -** The player who defends center field.

12. **CHARGE -** A rushing forceful attack.

13. **COVER -** To defend, protect, or shield from loss.

14. **CUT-OFF -** The interception by an infielder of a throw to second base, or to home plate from the outfield.

15. **FIELD -** An area in which an athletic event takes place.

16 **FIELDER -** He is the player who stands out in the field to catch, or stop balls.

17. **FIRST BASEMAN -** A baseball fielder responsible for the area near first base.

18. **GLOVE -** An over sized leather glove used for catching a baseball.

19. <u>**HIT -**</u> To come in contact with forcefully, to strike.

20. <u>**HOME PLATE -**</u> A five sided rubber slab at one corner of a baseball diamond at which a batter stands.

21. <u>**LEFT FIELDER -**</u> The player who defends left field.

22. <u>**LINE UP -**</u> **a.** They are members of a team chosen to start the game.
    b. The arrangement of persons when having a common purpose or sentiment, as to line-up a throw.

23. <u>**MISS -**</u> To fail to hit, reach, catch, meet, or other wise make contact with.

24. <u>**MOVE -**</u> To change position from one point to another.

25. <u>**OUT FIELD -**</u> In baseball the defensive position comprising right field, center field, and left field. Those are the players who occupy these positions.

26. <u>**PITCHER -**</u> The player who throws the ball from the mound to the batter.

27. <u>**PLAYER -**</u> A person who participates in or is skilled at some game.

28. <u>**RIGHT FIELDER -**</u> A player who defends right field.

29. <u>**RUN -**</u> **a.** Moving or going quickly.
    b. Moving swiftly on foot so that both feet leave the ground during each stride.
    c. In baseball this means to score.

30. <u>**SECOND BASE -**</u> The base across the diamond from home plate to be touched second by a runner.

31. <u>**SECOND BASEMAN -**</u> A player assigned to second base.

32. <u>**SHORTSTOP -**</u> The field position between second and third base.

33. <u>**STEP -**</u> **a.** It is the single complete movement of raising one foot and putting it down in another spot as in walking.
    b. A very short distance.

34. <u>**STOP -**</u> **a.** Halting the motion or progress of.

35. <u>**THIRD BASE -**</u> The base that must be touched third by a base runner in baseball.

36. <u>**THIRD BASEMAN -**</u> The player defending third base.

37. <u>**TOWARDS -**</u> In the direction of.

NOTES

About the Author

Charles R. Sledge Jr. was born on September 9th 1956 in a small town in Pittsburgh, Pennsylvania. He is the oldest son of three children. From the age of 8 yrs. old he has been an avid baseball player having a special love for the game. He played Little League, Pony League, and Colt League, High School and Semi-Pro baseball. Upon completion of High School, Charles attended college at the Art Institute of Pittsburgh where he became a professional artist. He landed a tryout with the Pittsburgh Pirates Baseball Club in 1975. He turns down an opportunity to play professional baseball to serve his country in the United States Army Infantry stationed in Berlin. He played semi-pro baseball for the Sea Side Bombers located on the west coast while in the army. His love for the game continued past his playing years. He married and became the father of four children, three boys and a girl. He volunteers his time coaching Little League Baseball in his home town. Charles has coached and managed all four children. To this date he is the manager and coach of the North Braddock Firemen Little League Team. He decided to write, and share what he has learned through the years with parents, coaches, and children everywhere. Charles wishes that you will get out of this manual all he put in.

Printed in the United States
147946LV00005B